Sandow Birk's

"In Smog and Thunder:

Historical Works from The Great War of the Californias"

Laguna Art Museum
Laguna Beach, California

in association with

Last Gasp
San Francisco, California

Curated by Tyler Stallings, Curator of Exhibitions

This book has been published in conjunction with *Sandow Birk's "In Smog and Thunder: Historical Works from The Great War of the Californias,"* curated by Tyler Stallings, Curator of Exhibitions, and organized by the Laguna Art Museum, Laguna Beach, California, where it was presented 16 April – 9 July 2000. The exhibition and book were made possible through the generous support of the William Gillespie Foundation, John Gunnin, Grand Central Art Center, Basil Alkazzi, Judy and Stuart Spence, Haim and Paula Schtrum, Jack and Susie Kenefick, Patsy Tartaglia, Janet and Henry Eggers, Richard McWilliam, Aileen and Bryan Cooke, Rene & Veronica di Rosa Foundation, Helene and Louis Galen, Angela Harrington, Marti Koplin, Jess H. Ghannam, Earl McGrath, Kay and George Birk, Catharine Clark, and Kristin and Greg Escalante.

Editor: **Cathy Curtis,** textual., Los Angeles, California
Designer: **Peter Morris,** Smashing Designs, La Jolla, California
Printed by: **Anthony Fowler / Rush Press**, San Diego, California

ISBN: 0-86719-497-9
All photographs courtesy of the artist unless otherwise credited.

The Spirit of Los Angeles, 1998. Oil on canvas, 54 x 43 inches. Courtesy Koplin Gallery, Los Angeles, California. ◦13◦

The Spirit of Los Angeles

Long thought lost and known only through images in contemporary magazines, this painting was recovered from the rubble of the artist's Hollywood studio during the Reconstruction. Heavily damaged, it was painstakingly restored for this exhibition.

Although not militarily accurate, or even relevant, this image nevertheless evoked that *je ne sais quoi* that unites all Angelenos and inspired the city in its darkest hours. Clearly intended as propaganda, with the loose brushwork typical of the times and a high school yearbook-style backdrop, this image nevertheless proved one of the most memorable and frequently reproduced of the war years.

Restoration was made possible by the limited exploitation of day laborers.

FRONT COVER IMAGE

BACK COVER IMAGE

The Wreck of the "Hollywood"

"Full fathom five thy father lies..."

Shakespeare's phrase seems to haunt the murky depths as submersibles descend to the muddy grave of the Hollywood. An age-crusted CHP cruiser and a jumble of traffic cones, like tombstones, litter the sea floor. Angeleno dreams of conquest vanished in a nightmare of crashing surf when the warship, her rudder smashed by the fury of Northern guns, was blown apart by her own munitions supply. In this artist's rendering, the ship still preserves the proud profile of her magnificent bow.

Despite forests of kelp and sand stirred by deep ocean swells that hampered visibility, a team of salvagers plumbing the turbulent waters recovered a priceless trove of relics.. The ship's weedy anchor was spotted by a pleasure diver nearly a mile from the site, where it rested in eighty feet of water. Winched up, the thirty-foot hook still held fragments of shrapnel. It now stands proudly at the entrance to the Seamen's Memorial at Point Fermin.

The Wreck of the "Hollywood" (detail), 2000. Oil on Canvas, 96 x 96 inches. Courtesy Koplin Gallery, Los Angeles, California.

Table of

contents

(the headphones symbol ⤜🎧⤛ throughout the catalogue denotes track number on accompanying CD)

The Bombardment of the
Getty Center

The monumental and well-guarded
edifices designed to preserve and
protect artistic and cultural icons
proved excellent defensive positions.
This image, reproduced extensively
in textbooks, clearly shows the
scale of efforts directed at capturing
the crucial Getty position. In the
foreground, Northern artillery fires
upon the heavily damaged structure,
while puffs of smoke from
Southern fire float from the
battlements. On the left, a platoon
of exhausted veterans watch
younger soldiers marching off in
preparation for an assault on the hill.

10

The Bombardment of the Getty Center, 1999. Graphite and Acrylic on Paper, 39 x 78 inches. Collection Jill and Jonathan Fink. ⟫11⟪

Foreword

The Laguna Art Museum is pleased to present *Sandow Birk's "In Smog and Thunder: Historical Works from The Great War of the Californias."* After viewing portions of it in exhibitions at the Catharine Clark Gallery in San Francisco and the Koplin Gallery in Los Angeles, we have decided to mount the first complete show of this hugely ambitious series. It has been only three years since Birk's last solo exhibition at the Museum, and we realize we're breaking what seems to be an unwritten law that artists should not be showcased more than once a decade. But we feel strongly that *The Great War of the Californias* needs to be seen in its entirety to be fully understood. Over the past few years, the depth and range of Birk's art has grown significantly, and we think it is important to validate such a major body of work made in our own backyard.

The Laguna Art Museum first showed Birk's work in 1992, in the group exhibition, *I Thought California Would Be Different.* The following year, he was included in another Museum show, *Kustom Kulture: Von Dutch, Ed "Big Daddy" Roth, Robert Williams & Others,* which traveled throughout the U.S. Birk's first solo exhibition at the Museum was *Carioca: A Year Among the Natives of Rio de Janeiro,* in 1997. Curated by Susan M. Anderson, it traveled to the San Jose Museum of Art. *Carioca,* a pseudoscientific documentation of typical inhabitants and everyday scenes in Rio de Janeiro, was inspired by Birk's Fulbright-sponsored visit to Brazil. His drawings and paintings parody the styles of early artist-explorers as a way of reconsidering the artist's role as a social critic. In *The Great War of the Californias,* Birk continues to reveal the blurred line between fact and fiction, history and imagination.

I am grateful to Museum staff members for making this exhibit possible: Tyler Stallings, Curator of Exhibitions, for initiating the project; Wendy Sears, Curator of Education, for creating a group of intriguing related events; Janet Blake, Curator of Collections/Registrar, for organizing loans from more than 80 collections and for the initial copyediting of the catalog; Ellen Girardeau Kempler, Communications Director, for spearheading a special, citywide radio campaign, a first for the Museum; and Mitch Goldstein, Exhibition Designer/Preparator, for helping to transform the main floor of the gallery into a facsimile of a nineteenth-century museum.

Additionally, I would like to thank the essayists, Claudine Isé and Marcia Tanner, for placing Birk's work within the context of art history and museology; Cathy Curtis for editing the catalog; and Peter Morris for designing the catalog, the first museum publication devoted entirely to Birk's art. Special thanks go to performer Paul Zaloom, who gave so much time from his busy schedule to collaborate with Birk on the CD audio tour.

We also are deeply indebted to: the William Gillespie Foundation for a generous grant that was instrumental in bringing the project to fruition; Basil Alkazzi for his generous support of the Museum and continuing support of Birk's vision; Grand Central Art Center Press in Santa Ana for their collaborative effort on the etching created as a fund-raiser for the exhibit; and Museum supporters Dr. Jess Ghannam, Angela and Gerald Harrington, Aileen and Bryan Cooke, Judy and Stuart Spence, Haim and Paula Schtrum, Janet and Henry Eggers, Jack and Susie Kenefick, Patsy Tartaglia, Richard McWilliam, Rene & Veronica di Rosa Foundation, Helene and Louis Galen, Kay and George Birk, Earl McGrath, Catharine Clark, Marti Koplin, and Kristin and Greg Escalante. Knowing there are numerous collectors who now have blank spaces on their walls where a favorite work used to hang, I want to give special thanks to all the lenders to the exhibition.

Laguna Art Museum's Board of Trustees deserve a separate thank-you for their loyal support of the Museum's artistic vision. In particular, LAM Board Trustee John Gunnin was instrumental in securing major support from the William Gillespie Foundation. Lastly, I want to thank Sandow Birk for sharing his vision with us.

Bolton Colburn, Director

Homeless Veterans Assistance Program, 1998. Acrylic on Paper, 38 x 25 inches. Courtesy Catharine Clark Gallery, San Francisco, California.

12

Artist's Acknowledgments

Remembering the darkest nights of the War and the distant, glimmering dawn of Peace over the rocky horizon, we must bow our heads in honor of the efforts of the few who have done so much for so many. From the mists, which obscure the countenances of many unnamed heroes, there emerge a few most deserving of a brighter beam of sunlight to illuminate their personal efforts and sacrifices.

Among those are: Tyler Stallings and Bolton Colburn, for their organizational efforts in bringing together this exhibition; Catharine Clark and her Fog Town gallery, for years of unflagging support, encouragement, and belief in my work; artists Stephen Rivers and Kevin Ancell, for their ideas and collaborations; Judy and Stuart Spence, for their years of support and encouragement; Eleana Del Rio and Marti Koplin, for their continuing support of my professional campaign; and Basil Alkazzi, for his friendship and generous award.

Communications were greatly enhanced by the efforts of Paul Zaloom, narrator, director, and producer of the audio scripts, whose enthusiastic devotion of time, energy, and humor was crucial. Audio technical skills – recording, engineering, and production — were provided by Eric Rathgerber and Cement Records. And I am deeply grateful to Peter Morris, designer of the catalog.

On the home front, victory would not have been assured without the ongoing support of the individual donors — whose financial assistance and personal sacrifices supplied our boys in combat until the very end — and my parents, whose understanding and patience has been unlimited.

And lastly, I must thank Lorena for her love and support through the darkest hours of the war, when victory seemed as distant as the farthest shores and the possibilities of defeat were as dire as the stormy waters of the deep Pacific. May she see me through many wars yet to come and finally into Arcadian fields.

Thank you all.

Sandow Birk
Seaman 1st Class, Artists' Corp., United Navy of the Californias

14

This book is dedicated to Jeffrey Brian Birk,
whose love of history would have made him
a great supporter of the cause.
Alas, he was one of its first casualties.

Introduction

An Introduction to The Great War of the Californias

by Sandow Birk

≥⋒≤

As a vapid populace mourned the voluntary retirement of its favorite sitcom, a thunderous and decisive war hovered on the western horizon, fed by clichés and confusion, fueled by bitterness and greed, and flavored with the pungent spices of myriad immigrant communities.

The Great War of the Californias was fought in a thousand places. From Lake Tahoe to Tijuana, in places like Potrero and Pasadena, Bakersfield and Beverly Hills, Telegraph Hill and Tarzana. More than three million Californians fought in it, and over 20,000 died in it. Californians killed each other in California towns, along California beaches, in California skies. In the two days of fighting at the Battle of Van Nuys, 2,000 died in a mere forty minutes.

Initially known as "The War of the Cities," "The Seven Months' War," and even "The Struggle Between Fog and Smog," the conflict soon developed a force and scale that no one had foreseen, and resulted in tragic episodes mourned and honored to this day.

The Great War rolled up an unlikely mixture of personalities, decisions, and actions into the giant burrito of history. It was to make some people rich and most people poorer, and to bestow celebrity on rank unknowns. Immigrants from more than 100 countries, many of them survivors of wars in their homelands, found themselves engaged in epic battles for their adopted land.

A struggling actress from Fresno, with nothing more notable on her résumé than a bit part in a failed soap opera, would mount a dramatic mobile assault. An immigrant Mexican laborer, with a love of gardening and a bad back, would lead 10,000 troops in one of the bloodiest battles of his adopted Southland.

The works in this exhibition represent only a portion of the vast record left by artists of the period. Although many were unschooled, they brought a sense of immediacy to the momentous events of their era. Individual canvases were chosen as much for their personal insights or unique viewpoints as for their artistic merits. Together, they tell a moving tale of national heroism, personal loss, and sacrifice.

This catalog is intended to provide historical context for the artworks, many of which have been loaned by the California War Museum in Tijuana. The organizers of this exhibition wish to thank them for their unflagging spirit of cooperation. We are also deeply indebted to generous grants from our corporate sponsors and the generous support of art patrons.

The Invasion of San Francisco

San Francisco on the Ruins of Her City

Painted in the months following the invasion, this tragic image of the City Herself has been reproduced on posters, calendars, T-shirts, and finally on the obverse of Northern currency. Poignant and emotional, it has been one of the most recognized images of the war since its unveiling at the Golden Gate Salons. The painting was an immediate success with an audience still struggling to make sense of the destructive events of the initial months of the war, and some scholars have pointed to it as one of the key elements in an increasing wave of Northern nationalism.

Yet, despite its renown, it proved to be the albatross of the artist's career. Although he continued painting for nearly a decade, he was never able to free himself from the tremendous success of this sentimental image. He languished in lesser galleries — despite a late-career switch to installation work and a brief stint as a drummer in an underground band — and finally died from an overdose in his downtown loft. ⋛⟨5⟩⋚

In early May of that tumultuous year, the South made its move. The plan was dramatic and decisive, and, in a tragic sense, brilliant.

General Juan Gomez de Los Angeles had been named Supreme Commander of the Southern Army only six months earlier, crowning a long and distinguished military career. After three months of secret preparations, he embarked on a daring and brilliant campaign that was to divide the people of California and shape the course of history.

An inversion layer blanketed the Southern basin as three Angeleno brigades began the march toward San Francisco. The first was led by General James Walker, who had lost his virginity unsatisfactorily at a Grateful Dead concert in his teens and despised the City ever since. The second was led by Commander Thomas Park, a former Los Angeles Raiders fan who had never forgiven the team for returning to Oakland. The third was led by Lieutenant Commander Alison Scott, a struggling actress hoping for the starring role that had always eluded her.

While Park and Scott conveyed the main body of the force up Interstate 5 and Walker moodily wandered off to visit his estranged wife in Tarzana, Gomez chose the scenic route along Highway 1. A day's march north of San Luis Obispo, he encountered his first setback. In Big Sur, a group of heavily armed hemp farmers mistook the soldiers for DEA agents, and a skirmish ensued. The vastly outnumbered farmers were quickly routed, but a few managed to escape to the City, where they spread word of Southern troops on the move. Tragically, their warning was not heeded, and those muffled shots on the craggy bluffs of Big Sur would mark the start of the Great War.

The Southern troops continued unopposed, through Pacifica and as far north as Daly City. "From that wretched suburb," Gomez wrote, "the whole of the City lay sparkling at my feet."

In the bay, Admiral Horatio Blake, furious at being taken by surprise in his home port, put up a courageous fight and sunk two Los Angeles ships near Alcatraz. Although his outdated fleet had trouble maneuvering in the wind, it managed to stall the invaders until the devastating arrival of the L.A. submarine, *The Gnarler.*

As the afternoon waned, Hwang met with her aides in a Chinatown dim sum shop. There she urged Lieutenant Mark Frye to push south and counterattack at Potrero Hill. Frye chose not to. Rather than attack and risk heavy bombardment, he dug in along Market Street.

By the end of the first day, the invaders controlled the heights in the South of Market neighborhood and Southern troops continued to make their way up Interstate 5. Hwang clung to the posh hills of the old City. Assigned to stabilize Telegraph Hill, Northern Lieutenant Quincy Salerno instead went on a drinking binge in North Beach. Ignoring orders and swearing vengeance against the Southern dogs, he abandoned the hills and recklessly led his troops into the flatlands of Valencia and Guerrero streets.

At mid-morning the following day, General Gomez and his Smog Battalions attacked from the Sunset district. Combining with reinforcements landing at the Marina, they pushed hard for Nob Hill. It was sparsely defended by a tenacious band of lesbians and Hispanic maids, whom the Southerners overran after a fierce struggle.

"From here," Gomez told Park in a specially encrypted cell phone conversation, "I can rain shells on the whole City."

Hwang immediately sent a brigade scrambling for Telegraph Hill to counterbalance Gomez's new position. When 300 San Franciscans reached the hill, artillery volleys shook the air. The attacking Southern troops surged up the side streets and alleys. In two hours, nearly a third of the defenders fell. Gunfire from Chinatown echoed ominously, and Hwang feared she would be surrounded.

"We are nearly out of ammunition and we are taking bullets from our fallen comrades," Hwang noted in her Palm Pilot. "The hour has come when we must either advance or retreat. It must not be the latter!"

Desperate, Hwang called for a daring and risky maneuver. Commanding the center to hold position, she ordered the left flank down the hill in counterattack. The speed of the assault stunned the Angelenos, many of whom turned and fled in confusion. As the afternoon waned, she managed to reconnect with Frye and form a new line around Geary Street and Union Square. By the end of the day, Fog Forces had captured nearly 4,000 Smog Boys, securing Telegraph Hill. It was a small victory in the midst of overwhelming defeat, but its importance in boosting morale could not be underestimated.

Two days later in Los Angeles, 100,000 people crowded the Plaza de la Raza to hear Vicente Fernandez sing "Caminos de Michoacán" and cheer the raising of the '49ers flag captured at Candlestick Park.

As the news of San Francisco's devastation spread to the Pacific Northwest, Portland poet and waiter Gary Amesbury was stunned. "Nothing we have known remains," he told a hushed crowd of regulars at Java Joe's. There was no doubt as to which way the Northwest would swing.

Before the Battle of San Francisco, only two generals in the Northern army had ever led a force into live combat, and the active troops numbered only 17,000. After Telegraph Hill, a newfound patriotism and government propaganda fueled recruiting efforts. Within two weeks, 10,000 citizens had joined the call to regroup, rebuild, and avenge their City.

Skirmishes and preemptive actions were erupting throughout the state. Just west of Fresno, a young general led his new recruits to secure the California Aqueduct to maintain local water supplies. The North seethed for revenge, and the stage was set for a new phase of war. Yet none could see the horrors that lay ahead.

Stop This Monster, 1998. Acrylic on Paper, 38 x 25 inches.
Courtesy Catharine Clark Gallery, San Francisco, California.

Los Angeles the Devourer, 1998.
Acrylic and Pencil on Paper, 38 x 25 inches.
Courtesy Catharine Clark Gallery, San Francisco, California.

Join the SFAF, 1998. Acrylic on Paper, 38 x 25 inches.
Collection Johnathon E. Powk

STOP THIS MONSTER!

>16< (all posters)

JOIN THE SFAF

Allegory of The Great War of the Californias

In this overtly romanticized portrayal, the cities of San Francisco and Los Angeles are seen in the throes of their epic struggle while the muses of the lesser towns lament and attempt to intervene. Images of this type were popular at the time—an era when a population hardened to the realities of a universally armed citizenry embraced melodramatic notions of heroism. >2<

Meanwhile, gas stations, mini-marts and fast food restaurants along Interstate 5 were overwhelmed by the needs of an army on the move. Many emporiums were soon out of beer and Fritos, and cash machines ran out of twenties. The stage was set for the bloodiest battle in California history.

The attack on an unsuspecting San Francisco came from three directions at once. Los Angeles ships under the command of Admiral B. Sousa bombarded Fort Point and the Golden Gate in an effort to isolate the City while Gomez's troops advanced along the coast, meeting no resistance. At Folsom Street, they turned east across the Sunset District, toward the City center. Homeless people in the shrubbery of Golden Gate Park called out unintelligible prophecies before disappearing into their cardboard condos. By noon, Park's three battalions were pushing toward Twin Peaks.

Meanwhile, Northern Brigadier General Susan Hwang and her rapidly mobilized Fog Forces lost precious hours securing the Embarcadero and the Bay Bridge, where they erroneously believed the assault on the City would begin.

Allegory of The Great War of the Californias, 1998. Oil on Canvas, 43 x 54 inches. Collection Eileen Natuzzi, M.D.

The Great
Battle of S. Francisco

The Battle of San Francisco

Northern forces and civilians alike hold the line against a fierce onslaught of Southern invaders in this richly detailed panorama depicting what journalist Charles Krasner called, "a turning point in history and in human destiny." While the battle rages, the fatally wounded General M. "Guitar" Frye can be seen amid the debris of the urban struggle.

The artist ingeniously adapted *plein-air* sketches made on the battlefield, superimposing a small but dramatic section of the mighty charge on the landscape background. In the distance, the full force of the first Southern assault can be seen on the Northern bulwarks.

The artist bathed the landscape in smoke -- an ominous black for the Southern artillery, and a billowing white for the City's — an overtly symbolic device by a painter who had served two years as a Northern gunner. ⇥④⇤

The Battle of San Francisco, 1996. Oil and Acrylic on Canvas, 84 x 84 inches. Collection Rene & Veronica di Rosa Foundation, Napa, California.

Rendezvous at Twin Peaks

Secure atop the heights of Twin Peaks, Southern commanders meet before ordering an artillery barrage against the City below. In the shelling that followed, the hilltops were obscured by a heavy fog bank — hardly enticing conditions for any painter.

Seemingly added as an afterthought, the clumsy and stunted characters in this stiffly academic painting have been likened to cardboard cut-outs. While the war proved to be the crucial event in the careers of major artists, it also impelled less-talented painters and draftsmen to produce images for a populace longing to see key events of their era recorded for posterity. In the wave of memorializing activity that washed across an ever-patriotic population, the monstrous events of urban conflict often were distorted in an effort to make them seem more meaningful.

Despite the painting's flaws, it is interesting to note the unusual depiction of a supply-line taco truck, representing a reality of warfare rarely depicted in more heroic images. ⊰❻⊱

Rendezvous at Twin Peaks, 1996. Oil and Acrylic on Canvas, 50 x 50 inches. Collection Paul Stephen Price.

"Memorial to the Great Battle of San Francisco," 1996. Oil and Acrylic on Canvas, 54 x 34 inches.
Collection Ryszard Koprowski

The Bombardment of Fort Point, 1996. Oil and Acrylic on Canvas, 34 x 57 inches.
Collection Peter Blumberg

"San Franciscan" – The Seas Are Ours!, 1998. Acrylic on Paper, 38 x 25 inches. Collection Isabel and David Breskin.

26

The War at Sea

The Final Hours of Telegraph Hill, 1996. Oil and Acrylic on Canvas, 43 x 54 inches. Collection Barbara DeZonia.

San Franciscans felt a profound sense of devastation and loss following the invasion. Never before had their great city been so wounded and their beliefs so deeply shaken. And yet, in the midst of this gloomy aftermath, the City already was plotting its revenge.

With a smaller population and fewer resources, the generals of San Francisco pinned their hopes on the navy, mothballed in the depths of the Oakland shipyards. By capitalizing on their superior naval history, the City hoped to shift the war to the high seas.

On a Sunday afternoon in late summer, San Francisco ships slipped out of the Golden Gate and steamed south. Almost fifty vessels strong, from troop-transporting tugs to mighty destroyers, the Northern navy had been refitted and rebuilt in a mere four months.

A nearly forgotten carrier had been hastily refurbished to become the mighty flagship, *The San Francisco.* Approximately 1,200 feet from bow to stern, she easily fitted forty-three attack fighter jets and eighty-three guns on her massive decks. Towering fifteen stories, she was the largest war vessel of her day, and carried a full crew of 733. Reborn after a peaceful retirement, she was to lead the largest naval assault in California history.

Admiral Chauncey Metcalf's plan called for the more powerful frigates and destroyers to swing west and south, and use the Channel Islands as cover to capture the sleeping Angeleno fleet in Long Beach harbor. While the larger ships engaged the enemy, a fleet of smaller craft would land 15,000 men at Hermosa and Manhattan beaches. It was a daring plan, and Metcalf was determined to attain it, or lose his other leg trying.

The Destruction of the LAS "Tinsel Town" by the SFS "Republic of San Francisco", 1998. Oil on Canvas, 24 x 48 inches. Collection Christopher Gaebler.

The Destruction of the LAS "Tinsel Town" by the SFS "Republic of San Francisco"

As both the title and exaggerated perspective suggest, this depiction of the famous sea battle is presented from the Northern point of view. Among the innumerable period depictions of this event off the Channel Islands, the artist has chosen a dramatic, sea-level viewpoint. At the peak of the battle, according to an eyewitness account, "the *Tinsel Town* careened heavily to the starboard from the effects of shot holes on her waterline." Its demise sounded a death knell for the slow and heavy ships of her era. ⇒〈67〉⇐

But the weather did not cooperate. Winds and currents sent the convoy further west than Metcalf had intended, and unusually dense summer fog lingered around Point Conception, making the inside passage through the Channel Islands forbiddingly treacherous. Orders were given to swing out to sea and skirt the islands. But Metcalf, hard-headed and stubborn, kept his course through the narrow channel.

While most of the Southern fleet remained docked in Long Beach, a convoy of Angeleno ships under the young Admiral Pete Petelo huddled into the leeward side of Santa Cruz Island to wait out the fog. His rag-tag convoy of outdated frigates, schooners, and sailboats numbered but seventeen. Even his flagship, *The Pounder* — a three-decked, eighty-four-gun man-o'-war — been saved from the scrap yard only by its role as a movie prop in swashbuckling pirate romances.

As the fog suddenly lifted, *The San Francisco* suddenly found herself alone, separated from the fleet, and nearly surrounded by seventeen enemy ships. It was too late to launch the fighters, and the winds favored the Angelenos. Metcalf immediately ordered his seamen to open fire. By mid-afternoon the flagship was aflame, and by dusk she listed heavily to starboard but stubbornly refused to go down.

In Long Beach, a week after the battle, the parents of John Stavros learned that he was among those missing at sea. His fellow sailors were certain he had perished but were unable to recognize his swollen body bobbing in the cold waters of the Pacific. With a heavy heart, his father placed a headstone over an empty grave at the Sailors' Cemetery on Signal Hill.

In San Francisco, Corporal Alfred Hoskin's coffin came home to the Haight. He was buried with full honors in Golden Gate Park. After the final flag was run up in surrender, the Northern Lieutenant John Sanders went aboard the Southern ship *Pantages*, where he found his son, John Sanders Jr., mortally wounded on the deck. Tragically, Junior had enlisted only because he no longer could stand the humiliation of bussing tables. John Senior silently pocketed his son's tattered business card ("actor, model, whatever") as a memento of his short life.

The Triumph of "The San Francisco"

One of the most successful naval battle depictions of all time, this magnificent reconstruction evokes the desperation of the outdated Smog Town galleons about two hours after the Northern fleet, led by the looming flagship *The San Francisco*, had smashed through the ragged enemy line.

Though many artists have turned their talents to this episode, none have succeeded in recreating that major historical turning point more remarkably than this contemporary painter. It took the artist three years to finish this panoramic canvas, in which he not only depicts the peak moment of that bloody afternoon but also draws on countless eye-witness accounts (including Admiral Rodriguez' own unpublished notes).

The artist himself appears to have been satisfied with the results, save for one detail. A few years after it was hung in the United Officers' Club on Nob Hill, he asked permission to "lighten the picture" by adding another stretch of sky. Viewers may note the faintly visible band of discoloration along the top of the canvas that marks this addition.

Courtesy of the Veterans of California Wars Commission.

The Triumph of "The San Francisco," 1998. Oil on Canvas, 90 x 134 inches. Courtesy Catharine Clark Gallery, San Francisco, California.

Portrait of Lt. Quincy Salerno, 1996. Oil and Acrylic on Canvas, 30 x 22 inches. Collection Jess H. Ghannam.

Portrait of Gen. Felix Hernandez, 1998.
Oil and Acrylic on Canvas, 30 x 22 inches. Collection Basil Alkazzi.

Portrait of Lt. Comdr. Rebecca Jordan, 1998. Oil on Canvas, 30 x 22 inches. Collection Jess H. Ghannam.

Gallery of

Portrait of Lt. Maj. DJ Down, 1998. Oil on Canvas, 30 x 22 inches. Collection Paul and Jill Koplin.

Portrait of Maj. Gen. Juan Gomez de los Angeles, 1996. Oil and Acrylic on Canvas, 30 x 22 inches. Courtesy Koplin Gallery, Los Angeles, California.

Portrait of Col. Don Ho Park, 1998. Oil on Canvas, 30 x 22 inches. Courtesy Koplin Gallery, Los Angeles, California.

Heroes

For the City, My Eyes... Angelenos Unite, 1998. Acrylic on Paper, 38 x 25 inches. Collection Philip E. Thomas.

32

The Great Battle of Los Angeles

Los Angeles Triumphant, 1998. Oil on Canvas, 54 x 43 inches. Collection Donald R. Boulanger.

Los Angeles Triumphant

In this symbolic painting, intended both to commemorate battlefield glories and boost Smog Town morale, the muse of Los Angeles is represented by a pregnant Latina, adorned with the coat of arms of her city as she treads on an image of the disgraced Raiders, whose earlier return to the North had become synonymous with betrayal. Scholars have noted that, as the city's population became increasingly Hispanic, the Galaxy became widely known as L.A.'s football team. ≥⟨19⟩≤

Just 204 days after the devastating Battle of San Francisco, the City regrouped and came howling back for revenge: Storming out of the purple dusk in SUVs and minivans, the rapid deployment force cut a roaring swath of destruction through the San Fernando Valley. Burning and looting as they came, they were hell-bent on obliterating the hated foe.

The initial attack proved surprisingly easy. After a long political struggle, the Valley had recently seceded from the City of Los Angeles. In Woodland Hills and Westlake, scattered troops fell back before the onslaught, firing just a few token shots in defense.

Valley generals convened in a hastily organized meeting near the Galleria. Many argued that assistance from Los Angeles would be required to hold off the attack. Yet others who came to power after the secession could not bear to rely on the city they had worked so hard to leave behind.

From his bunker headquarters beneath the Hollywood Hills, a bitter General Gomez watched the Valley burn. "Let it go," he reportedly told his aides. "Let the bastards burn."

The buffer zone of the doomed Valley gave Gomez time to organize resistance by cell phone. Lieutenant Felix Hernandez was the first man on his list. A tough and determined leader on the Westside, he was ordered to round up as many of his men as he could and carve out a stand at the Sepulveda Pass.

From the high ground at the Getty Center, a few hundred Angeleno troops held ten freeway lanes against 5,000 San Franciscans. Hernandez's heroic stand stalled the Northern drive into L.A. and gave Park the extra hours he needed to creep down the 101 Freeway. He, too, held the high ground, at Cahuenga Pass. He brilliantly positioned his artillery the length of Mulholland Drive to command the approaches from the Valley, now smoldering in ruins.

As dusk fell, the triumphs on the hills contrasted with the sorry lot of the scattered Smog Town fleet, the imminent danger posed by the Fog Forces' push into Compton, and the exhaustion of the scrappy band led by General Skip Ramirez. In the heat of a stage-two smog alert, after losing nearly a third of his men the previous day, he and his thirsty troops were obliged to spend the night on the garbage-strewn hillside of Chavez Ravine. The next day brought the ignominy of a forced march through Glendale and Atwater, routed by Captain Chun Yeong Chang's tireless battalion of eleven-year-old computer programmers.

From Gomez's command post, the situation grew increasingly desperate. Fleeing Angeleno civilians looted each others' homes and major chain stores, so as to leave nothing of value for the advancing San Franciscans. Troops used the empty Beverly Center as a medical base, with supplies rescued from the devastated Cedars-Sinai Medical Center.

As Smog Town troops retreated through Downtown, traffic was gridlocked and the subways finally were useful to a terrified population. Mini-malls — earlier converted into impromptu forts — were trashed and abandoned. Famished families waited in long lines at Tommy's Burgers. A desperate group of Angelenos defending the Disney Symphony Hall quarreled so violently over the building design that they were easily routed by the northern army.

By afternoon the exhausted San Franciscans reached MacArthur Park. "The dead lay strewn among the homeless from Bonnie Brae to Figueroa," Chang would write on his home page. "But the dead do not ask for quarters."

It was at Vermont Avenue, however, that the tide began to turn. Disoriented Fog Town commanders were forced to rely on maps to the stars' homes purchased at roadside stands along their march. When Chang unexpectedly found himself in the midst of a Central American neighborhood, he soon lost all sense of direction, disoriented in the flat land by the spicy aromas of *empanadas* and *pupusas*.

By the weekend, Los Angeles was in desperate straits. Refugees were swelling the population, school buildings reeked with contamination, and there were no big hits so far in the fall TV season. At UCLA, fraternities burned Tommy Trojan in effigy and the price of cocaine hit $125 an ounce. Along the Miracle Mile, smog-alert conditions and the smoke from countless fires brought tears to the eyes of the most valiant veterans.

Fearsomely buffeted by the Northern reinforcements and threatened with a SAG strike, General Gomez was at his wits' end. Air defenses were in tatters, the navy had been defeated, and he was receiving intelligence reports that Portland and Seattle were sending reinforcements to the San Francisco forces. Even his last-ditch strategy of enlisting Las Vegas in the southern struggle had collapsed.

"We regret to inform you that we cannot be of service in your predicament," a consortium of casino owners replied in a form letter that misspelled Gomez's name. "However, we have enclosed a coupon for three free spins at our $10 roulette."

After extensive but fruitless negotiations, Orange County and San Diego had both decided to remain neutral. Arrogantly overconfident, the kingdom of suburban tract houses and theme parks turned a blind eye to the sufferings of its more cosmopolitan neighbor. Busy with shopping and tennis, residents failed to perceive the threat looming behind clouds of war. Similarly, the San Diego population was too preoccupied by maniacal fence-building on the Mexican border to comprehend the threat of an invasion from the north.

Of all the territories with which Angelenos pleaded for assistance, only Tijuana offered its support. On the eve of 24 August, she rose brilliantly to the challenge. Long-suffering Baja California sent wave upon wave of skilled guerrilla fighters whose bravery and intimate

 (all posters)

knowledge of the terrain turned the tide of the war. In the final draft of the peace accord, politicians voted resoundingly (119 to 56) to abolish the southern border of the Californias.

But victory brought scarcity in its wake. Water, when it could be found, cost $14 a gallon. The price of *carne asada* rocketed to $22 a pound, and three-day rentals at Blockbuster were as much as $36 for new releases.

During the celebrations attending the peace agreements, the crowd called out to Gomez to speak. Too exhausted to approach the podium, he refused. Instead, he asked the band to play a solemn rendition of "I Left My Heart in San Francisco." The Angelenos, many of whom were already planning bed-and-breakfast vacations in Fog City or plotting joint ventures with Silicon Valley dot-com start-ups, roared with delight. Whereupon Park rose and called for more somber celebrations.

"We are all Californians," he said. "And no one is the victor."

Meanwhile, in San Francisco, an old friend found General Susan Hwang in her room and asked her if she wanted to go for a drink. "Yes," she replied slowly, a far-away glint in her eye. "Anything to bring back the fog that I love so dearly. And make it a tequila with lime."

The Three Headed Monster of the North, 1998. Acrylic on Paper, 38 x 25 inches.
Lynn and John Pleshette Collection.

The Great Battle of Los Angeles

Although grandiose in scale and
monumental in vision, this image
is but a preparatory sketch for the
famous cyclovision panorama painting
of the Battle of Los Angeles now on
permanent view at the California
War Museum in Tijuana.

The artist took nearly four years to
complete what would be one of the
most technically accurate views of
the devastating climax of the
event, based on personal accounts
and interviews with veterans of the
engagement. Despite certain
inadequacies as a portrait
painter— many of the foreground
figures have similar features, and
some have none at all — the artist
painstakingly introduced such
arresting details as the blood-
spattered laptops and the rallying
of theme park employees caught
up in the struggle. A pamphlet
that accompanied engraved copies
of the painting explained that the
artist spent "weeks at the battle-
ground transcribing the portraiture
of the field to canvas."

When Commander L. Rodriguez
first saw this canvas, she declared
it "wonderfully accurate in its
delineation of the landscape and
position of the troops . . . a
remarkably fair and complete
representation" of that eventful
scene. "There," she said pointing
to the charred remains of a phone
booth, "is where I came to grief."

36

The Great Battle of Los Angeles, 1998. Oil and Acrylic on Canvas, 64 x 120 inches.
Collection Louis and Helene Galen.

Air Supremacy, 1998. Oil on Canvas, 32 x 22 inches. Collection Dean Ziehl.

Air Supremacy

Although they were slow-moving and lightly armed, zeppelins were valued for their appeal to advertisers targeting specific audiences as well as for military deployment. Long used as spotters to coordinate defenses from their lofty vantage points, they were secretly dreaded by fighter pilots worried about getting tangled up in their dangling lines and cables.

One of many depictions of zeppelin battles in the Great War, this image of two blimps dog-fighting over the Southland is a remarkable tribute to the airmen who flew them. After hanging for several years in the Royal Angeleno Airmen's League, the painting was vandalized by a knife-wielding San Francisco Pepsi drinker, now serving time in Soledad penitentiary, midway between the two metropolises. Restoration was made possible by a grant from the Coca-Cola Bottlers' Association. ⇒〖14〗⇐

The Bombardment of San Pedro

In this contemporary depiction, the wrecks of ships sunk in the attack on San Pedro loll in the shallows, and smoke from bombardments billow from the hills of Palos Verdes during the Battle of Los Angeles. Fierce, an Angeleno sub, slips out of Long Beach while anti-aircraft fire explode among the trails of aerial dogfights. Smog Towns experience and expertise at deception and conniving were key characteristics in the success of Operation Back-Stab, which relied heavily on sub-surface tactics and Hollywood insiders. A similar version of this scene hangs at the California War Museum in Tijuana, along with several scenes on black velvet by this outstanding artist.

L.A. Story: *Sandow Birk's "In Smog and Thunder: Historical Works from The Great War of the Californias"*

by Claudine Isé

History painting may have been out of fashion for centuries, but Sandow Birk has single-handedly revived the genre with his series of works that recount a fictitious war between Northern and Southern California, nicknamed "Fog Town" and "Smog Town," respectively. Consisting of military portraits, battle scenes, drawings, aerial maps, political posters, and model ships, *In Smog and Thunder: Historical Works from The Great War of The Californias* is at once an outright hoax and an ambitious work of historical and museological fiction. Skillfully exploiting the conventions of museum display that tether belief to that which is presented as "fact," Birk's works are framed by a network of

didactic wall texts, sketches and diagrams, and even an Acoustiguide tour. Collectively, these pedagogical tools activate the entire exhibition space in the service of an elaborately sustained lie. Although viewers know from the get-go that this account of the Great War cannot be accurate, the conflicts portrayed in Birk's paintings clearly reflect many of the material and social realities that confront Californians today.

Making porous the barrier between history and myth, fact and fiction, Birk's profoundly unhistorical history paintings never seem more perversely "truthful" than when they are stoking our fears and fantasies of a Los Angeles hurtling toward imminent doom. L.A. has the distinction of being both the entertainment capital of the world and, in the minds of many, the most disaster-prone city in the nation. Fires, floods, earthquakes, riots, and a couple of sensationalistic murder trials have provided the rest of the country with some of the most dramatic and controversial (not to mention entertaining) news stories in recent memory. Indeed, the paintings that comprise Birk's Battle of Los Angeles series implicitly acknowledge the fact that L.A.'s most pressing political, social, and ecological crises seem at times to double as mass-media "content," providing network news programs with real-life urban sagas, staged for the nation's voyeuristic delectation.

Birk's paintings take the form of battle scenes, allegorical tableaux, and military and equestrian portraits borrowed from history paintings by Jacques-Louis David, Eugène Delacroix,

The End of the Siege of the Getty, 1998. Ink on Paper, 17 x 14 inches. Collection Patricia Minatoya.

Théodore Géricault, Francisco Goya, and Antoine-Jean Gros. For example, David's *Napoleon Crossing the Alps* provides the inspiration for Birk's *Portrait of Col. Don Ho Park*; Delacroix's *Liberty Leading the People (28 July 1830)* serves as the model for Birk's *The Spirit of Los Angeles*, and Gros's portrait of Joachim Murat inflects Birk's *Portrait of Maj. Gen. Juan Gomez de Los Angeles*. As in the paintings of David and other neoclassicists, Birk's subjects are restrained in facial expression and physical gesture. The pictorial space is shallow, with figures arranged in frozen tableaus. In Birk's works, however, past and present intersect in witty and often jarringly anachronistic ways. Soldiers ride horses and Harley-Davidsons. Helicopters patrol the air, surveying the smoky ruins of the city below, while the sea is commandeered by submarines as well as clipper ships and other sailing vessels, their masts emblazoned with logos for Visa and MasterCard.

Didactic panels describe the trajectory of each battle and detail the events leading up to the war, which, we are informed, was "as much an economic and industrial conflict as an armed struggle." Although the Fog Towners suffer initial losses during the Battle of San Francisco, they fight back by ingeniously capitalizing on their enemy's blind spot. When Fog Town battalions are stymied by traffic jams on the 10 Freeway, they turn the tables on their foes by staging a surprise invasion through the Port of Los Angeles, surmising correctly that the hapless Smog Towners, oblivious to the seaport's existence, would be taken completely unawares. As the Fog Towners press further into Los Angeles, the Smog Towners recruit additional troops from Tijuana to help stem the advancing tide.

When the military situation grows dire, Smog Town leaders ask Hollywood to provide them with extras to replenish the troops. The twisted logic that lies within this hyperreal scenario is not likely to be lost on today's media-savvy viewer. Films like *Wag the Dog* — in which a presidential spin doctor hires a famous Hollywood producer to stage a phony war with a fictional country to distract the nation from the commander in chief's sexual dalliances — suggest that in an age where politics, media, and entertainment are blurred, the only battle that needs to be fought is over airtime. As postmodern theorist Jean Baudrillard might put it, if a war isn't covered by CBS, NBC, ABC, and CNN, it never really happened.

Jacques-Louis David and other history painters are in many respects the forebears of today's Hollywood producers and directors. In his time, David was something of an operator: openly competitive and often graspingly ambitious, he was an expert schmoozer who often incurred the resentment of his fellow painters for the political dexterity with which he manipulated patrons and public alike. Above all, David wanted to make the world understand that painting was a great, noble, and necessary pursuit. He meticulously researched his subjects to ensure that his costumes and settings were historically accurate in every detail. He used pupils, friends, and even his children's nurse as actors, "directing" them to assume various poses until he had arranged his scenes exactly as he wanted them. A staunch supporter of the French Revolution, David believed that art had a moral and educative purpose; he saw history painting as an avenue for public discourse, a means of shaping public opinion about the explosive political issues of the day. As such, his depictions of noble personages and heroic deeds from ancient and contemporary history helped foster a nascent bourgeois public sphere in revolutionary France.

The Desperate Charge of the 101, 1998. Ink on Paper, 17 x 14 inches. Courtesy Catharine Clark Gallery, San Francisco, California.

The more things change, the more they stay the same. More than 200 years later, Sandow Birk takes old master paintings and remakes them, in a manner not unlike a Hollywood director who sets out to translate Shakespeare to film or remake a classic movie. In the process, Birk demonstrates that the broad strokes and propagandistic overtones of classical history paintings are echoed in Hollywood's propensity for over-the-top narratives and the news media's sound-bite approach to reportage. Birk's decimated urban landscapes—strewn with Slurpees and Big Gulps, soccer balls, spray cans, skateboards, and other consumer detritus—also ask us to take stock of the ways in which today's public sphere, far from being an arena for meaningful public discourse and debate, has instead become a marketplace for an endless variety of consumer goods. The heroic personages that Birk depicts double as corporate pitchmen hawking a dizzying array of products. Instead of military camouflage, Birk's soldiers wear Dodger jackets, baseball caps bearing the Bud Light beer logo, and tee shirts emblazoned with the Domino's Pizza emblem. The war itself is sponsored by the likes of Nike and McDonald's, whose eponymous logos, emblazoned on banners and blimps, sail high above the burning city. *Los Angeles Triumphant* depicts a pregnant Latina, dressed in jeans, tank top, and flip-flops, clutching a skateboard in one hand and an Oscar in another. Above her head float two rococo cherubs holding a pair of Mickey Mouse ears in place of a halo.

Birk replaces the neoclassicists' all-white casts with a multiethnic array of hip, street-wise characters, re-staging the action in settings that reflect today's gritty urban realities. Birk's *Allegory of The Great War of the Californias*, for example, updates one of David's most dramatic paintings, *The Intervention of the Sabine Women*. David's 1799 masterpiece recounts the story of the Sabine women, who were abducted from their village by Romulus and his Romans to increase the population of their own city. The kidnapped Hersilia stands with outstretched arms

between her husband, Romulus, and her father, Tatius. As Hersilia begs them to lay down their weapons, other townswomen try to stop the melee by raising their infant children high in the air or placing them at the soldiers' feet. David's painting was unusual in its emphasis on passivity and forgiveness in the face of savage violence; significantly, it was also the first of his history paintings to feature a woman as its central figure. In Birk's hands, David's tableau becomes a desperate plea for peace made by the War's bit players—Bakersfield, Fresno, Santa Barbara, and Irvine—caught in the middle of the North-South conflict. Each of these cities is represented by a woman (Santa Barbara wears a skimpy bikini), with Santa Cruz as the central mediating figure. Arms akimbo, she stands directly between two men, one of whom holds a steering wheel and a miniature palm tree while the other grips a Slurpee and a tiny redwood tree.

Like all good satirists, Birk's underlying intentions are serious. His paintings make reference to many of Southern California's hot-button political issues, implicitly acknowledging the fact that long-simmering tensions, left unresolved, eventually will rip communities apart. It would be difficult indeed for any Angeleno to view Birk's depictions of Los Angeles in flames without immediately recalling the 1993 uprisings and their smoldering aftermath. The uprisings made it impossible to ignore the stark economic differences that divide Los Angeles into a city of rich and poor, with disproportionately large numbers falling into the latter category. Most of the damage occurred in

The Skater's Confession, 1998. Ink on Paper, 17 x 14 inches. Collection Kevin King.

South Central Los Angeles (seven years later, the area still has not rebounded economically), and for many Angelenos, particularly those living in wealthier Westside communities, the uprisings were experienced more as a televised spectacle than as an actual threat.

A number of other Southern California political and cultural battles find their way into these paintings. In Birk's fictional war, the often acrimonious San Fernando Valley secession movement proves to be the Valley's undoing when, as a wall label notes, the newly independent Valley residents refuse to ask for or accept aid from the city, and as a result are left "a smoldering ruin" by the invading Fog Town troops. The Smog Town forces rally after this major defeat and, led by General Felix Hernandez, secure key positions at the Sepulveda Pass directly below the Getty Museum. *Portrait of Gen. Felix Hernandez* depicts the general during a pensive moment. Standing alone at the Sepulveda Pass, Hernandez holds a leaf blower with one hand and a rake with the other; a *Thomas Guide*, binoculars, and laptop computer lie at his feet. As he gazes contemplatively into the distance, he seems to be weighing the backbreaking labor of his past against the hopeful yet uncertain benefits that new technologies will yield. This painting clearly makes reference to a controversial recent L.A. City Council ordinance that banned the use of leaf blowers within 500 feet of a residential area. L.A.'s gardeners are now legally required to use rakes, which not surprisingly slows down the rate at which they can complete their yard work. As a result of the ban, gardeners now can expect to be paid much less for doing far more work, a crippling economic blow to laborers who already are struggling to support their families. In 1998, a group of gardeners staged a hunger strike to protest the ordinance.

Another heroic leader of the Smog Town forces is the flamboyantly tricked-out, rapper-revolutionary DJ Down. *Portrait of Lt. Maj. DJ Down (The Battle of Los Angeles)* portrays Down straddling an L.A.P.D. motorcycle while outfitted in a bright red shirt, a pink-plumed pirate hat, an eye patch, and a gold earring. Backed by his Quickdraw Posse, Down "holds the high ground" at the Sepulveda Pass, while above them in the distance the Getty Museum is engulfed in flames. This painting riffs on the perceptions, held by some, that the Getty's elevated location makes it hard to visit and that it is a monument to cultural elitism. At the same time, the image of the Getty in flames also harks back to Ed Ruscha's *The Los Angeles County Museum on Fire* (1965-68), a painting made in the wake of the 1965 Watts riots. Hovering around the edges of Birk's "Great War" are memories of that conflagration, and, more recently, the traumatic civil uprisings that erupted in 1993 after four L.A.P.D. officers were acquitted of beating motorist Rodney King.

Birk's paintings beam California's social and political conflicts through an anamorphic lens, stretching some to exaggerated proportions while zeroing in on others with astonishing precision and clarity. His speculative fictions presage a tumultuous future that is already taking shape—a revolution that not only will be televised, but also will be cybercast, sponsored by Visa and Pepsi, and made into a TV movie of the week.

Claudine Isé is assistant curator at the UCLA/Armand Hammer Museum. She has written for the *Los Angeles Times, Art.issues, Artweek*, and other publications.

43

The Last Stand in the Marina, 1996. Ink on Paper, 15 x 12 inches. Collection Judy and Sheldon Greene.

A Museum of the Mind: Sandow Birk's "The Great War of the Californias"

by Marcia Tanner

And it's one, two, three, what are we fighting for?
— Country Joe MacDonald

Have fun. If not, you'll bore us.
— Marcel Duchamp

In his book *Circus Americanus*, art critic Ralph Rugoff considered the "museumization" of America, a phenomenon he observed after moving to Los Angeles in 1983 to report on the art and visual culture of Southern California.

"Beyond the influence of mass media and automobiles," he wrote, "an earlier technology seemed even more central to its evolving visual attitudes — namely, the museum vitrine. California . . . was home to a growing epidemic of museums." By the early 1990s, "this burgeoning museum culture was evident in most areas of the US, and . . . an obsession with looking at artifacts preserved under glass had replaced spectator sports as our national pastime."[1]

Rugoff was interested not only in these museums' collections, but "in the psychology of display, in what it reveals about the work of constructing, and reconstructing, history." Southern California seemed to be heading toward a future in which the museum's "institutionalized way of looking" would penetrate every facet of life. The region, he thought, was leading the way in a "general . . . shift . . . toward a culture of alienated spectacle where all aspects of experience, from shopping to warfare, are routinely transformed into thematized entertainment." While acknowledging the museum as an "ideological apparatus and paradigm of institutional power," Rugoff appreciated its "peculiar, and often delirious, poetics."[2]

At precisely this intersection of fantasy and power, Sandow Birk has constructed — within an actual art museum — a faux history museum dedicated to a fictional historic event, or perhaps to a prescient vision of a future event destined to become history. In *Smog and Thunder: Historical Works from*

The Oath of Allegiance, 1998. Ink on Paper, 17 x 14 inches. Collection Mike Merell.

The Great War of the Californias is a museological extravaganza: an "alienated spectacle . . . [of] thematized entertainment" *par excellence*. Full of laughs, thrills, and chills, it's as much Cecil B. DeMille-meets-*Blade Runner* and AOL-meets-Time Warner as the-Prado-meets-the-Louvre.

For this epic conceptual project, the artist created every object on view — paintings, drawings, political propaganda posters, models, maps, and other artifacts (all ostensibly made by diverse hands) — and also cast himself in the role of curator and institutional interpreter. Via labels, legends, wall texts, an audio tour, and the works themselves, Birk documents an apocalyptic civil war between Northern and Southern California.

Part One records the terrible battle in which Fog Town (S.F.) defends itself against an all-out military invasion by Smog Town (L.A.). Part Two chronicles Smog Town's valiant defense against Fog Town's surprise counterattack by sea. While both sides inflict hideous bloodshed and wholesale devastation on each other, the war's actual causes are mysterious and its outcome appears unresolved.

The cities are depicted as total war zones. There is violent hand-to-hand combat in the streets, demolition of cultural landmarks (SFMOMA, the Getty Center, Taco Bells and Pizza Huts), battles at sea and in the air. Military leaders are folk heroes who've clearly risen through the ranks. The "troops" are motley, untrained militias of multiethnic men and women: street people, surfers, skateboarders, gang bangers, bike messengers, and other urban warriors, haphazardly armed with an eclectic collection of often primitive weapons.

Combat vehicles range from horses and motorcycles to World War II tanks and jeeps. Naval engagements pit twentieth-century submarines and armored battleships against tri-masted sailing ships. Zeppelins engage helicopters and B-2 bombers in aerial combat, and catapults compete with Trident missiles. Both armies are underwritten by corporate sponsors — Nike, MasterCard, HBO, VISA, NBC and CBS — rather than governments, which may account for the apparently *ad hoc* military strategy of the campaigns.

Birk's *Historical Works* parody the compositions, styles, and techniques of historically iconic paintings and political posters, which themselves were often cast as allegories based on earlier depictions of vignettes from classical and Biblical tales, and were in turn co-opted by the Hollywood film industry for purposes of its own. Birk recruits early nineteenth-century British maritime battle scenes, panoramic war compositions by Albrecht Altdorfer, portraits by Diego Velasquez, etchings by Francisco Goya, and canvases by French neoclassical and Romantic painters Eugène Delacroix, Théodore Géricault, and Jacques-Louis David for his mock-heroic free-for-all.

The works reference an even wider range of visual sources. Birk cites an encyclopedic list of other art historical influences: European academic painters; works by British and American war artists (from Thomas Hart Benton's World War II naval paintings and Henry Moore's drawings of London in the Blitz through depictions of the recent Falklands War); German social satirists from George Grosz to Jorg Immendorf; the Russian Social Realists; Japanese woodcuts; and the U.S. Navy's collection of combat art.

Birk quotes imagery and visual vocabularies from popular, folk, and mass media culture: German graphic design; British World War II posters; Norwegian scrimshaw; French and Mexican comic books; Napoleonic-era miniatures; *Surfing Magazine;* advertisements and commercials; and model railroads built by contemporary hobbyists. Los Angeles culture also shapes Birk's magpie sensibility. Surfing, skateboarding, Hollywood, punk rock, and the street life of the predominately

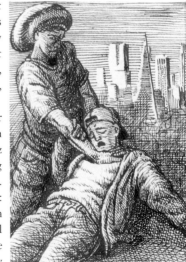

45

The Revenge of San Francisco, 1996. Ink on Paper, 8 x 6 inches. Collection J.O. Bugental.

Latino neighborhood in L.A. where he once lived intimately inform his work.

Unlike Mark Tansey, who also parodies historic European paintings, Birk isn't archly preoccupied with postmodern art-historical in-jokes. [3] Framing scenes of contemporary urban desolation, misguided machismo, and misdirected warfare in the exalted visual vocabularies he borrows is a strategy freighted with irony, but not just a cynical ploy.

Birk's historic pastiches are very much in the tradition of contemporary "bad" painting, characterized — in the words of Marcia Tucker — by "its refusal to adhere to anyone else's standards of taste or fashion, and its romantic and expressionistic flavor." For these artists, she writes, "content and form are used in a jarring juxtaposition that forces us to question not only how we see, but what we see and what kinds of image[s] we value. [4]

Birk skewers the grandiose pretensions and ideological agendas of those overblown yet masterfully executed and dramatically staged "great moments" in history. He sets up a disjunction between content, and style and execution that engages the viewer with historical resonance and visual richness, then delivers an intellectual, moral, and aesthetic double whammy with contemporary references and calculated awkwardness.

While the objects in Birk's museum co-opt the inflated visual rhetoric of history paintings and political agitprop, his interpretive texts mimic the reverential, *ex cathedra* tone and disembodied, authoritative diction of museum-speak. Both languages are forms of euphemistic and manipulative hyperbole. Yet Birk's "explanatory" verbal narratives frequently contradict each other, just as the paintings' grand style contradicts their actual content.

46

The tension between what's actually going on and the pious glosses of text and image is the subject of Birk's critique. History painters are undeniably the great spin doctors of civilization; they skew their visual chronicles to conjure versions of the past that flatter the establishments they serve. Birk observes that history paintings "were *never* factual records of the events they portrayed. They were always more romantic, more beautiful, more morally correct, cleaner. People were painted in who weren't there. Times of day were altered for better light."

Museums, Birk says, "are generally the places that you go to find the 'truth' behind artworks." By presenting fictional materials as facts, he plays with the museum's role as purveyor of truth while questioning the notion of "truth" itself. [5] Birk is certainly not the first contemporary artist to deconstruct and subvert the conventions and assumptions of museum display. [6] But his *Great War* stakes out its own unique territory. It is a quintessentially Southern Californian take on the apparatus of disinformation, mass media infotainment, ideological propaganda, and the packaging of history, art, and all human experience as fictionalized spectacle, of which the excesses of museology are only one manifestation. To Birk, the museum is an emblem of the entire illusion industry, which arguably was perfected — if not invented altogether — in L.A., and has spread globally like a killer virus. A sprawling concatenation of tangible hallucinations, L.A. was the "society of the spectacle" long before that concept was a gleam in Guy Debord's consciousness.

The Arrival of Reinforcements on Lombard Street, 1996. Ink on Paper, 8 x 6 inches. Collection Kevin King.

Thanks to the globalization of American popular culture, the Los Angeles condition is fast becoming universal. In the apparent anachronisms and wildly anomalous juxtapositions of iconographic styles and content that permeate his work (Mickey Mouse waves a "Free ATM" banner in *The Great Battle of Los Angeles*, 1998), Birk is describing contemporary consciousness, which is not anachronistic but a-historic and pan-cultural: a state in which all human history and culture are instantly and simultaneously available to us and coexist in an undifferentiated space-time continuum. Anyone who grew up in L.A., where English Tudor, traditional Japanese, Mediterranean, French provincial, Bauhaus, and modern ranch houses stood side-by-side on the same suburban street, recognizes this mind-set. Angelenos viewed history as a theme park long before Disneyland, let alone the Internet.

Like Disneyland, Birk's work is characterized by its excesses: "bad" taste, hyperbole, primitivism with pretensions toward high art, and kitsch. But he adopts these as deliberate aesthetic strategies. *The Great War* is parody through and through. As Marcia Tucker has observed, "Parody is . . . used by artists to express the inexpressible, to create a formal and psychological imbalance which will counterpoint the corresponding paradoxes and schisms within the society in which the works were created."[7]

Birk's *Great War* is an extended travesty based on an elaborate, and transparent, prevarication: a Big Lie in the tradition of the American tall tale, whose phoniness is so self-evident that it becomes the point of the exercise.

Revealing truth through fiction is the artist's task, and Birk challenges the spectacle with a counter-spectacle of his own. He treads on sensitive ground here. We Americans are sentimental about our relatively shallow past even as we trash it. We tend to exaggerate and glorify what little history we do have, and fabricate what we lack.

"Cathedrals of iconic reassurance" is Umberto Eco's term for the small museums, crammed with replicas and "almost real" displays and artifacts, that pepper the American landscape.[8] Finding them symptomatic of "the constant 'past-izing' process carried out by American civilization in its alternate process of futuristic planning and nostalgic remorse," he notes "the kitsch reverence that overwhelms the visitor, thrilled by his encounter with a magic past."[9]

A fake "cathedral of iconic reassurance," Birk's *Great War* was inspired by the artist's visits to Civil War museums, and by his reading of war history books from many different eras. As he explains:

> I wanted to recreate the overall feeling of a Civil War museum, [where] the actual facts of the story of the war are secondary to the images. Using the Civil War as a model, I wanted to recreate the somber mood, the sense of heroism and honor of those places, and, importantly, the implication that the war is something that is well-known and understood. I saw the project as more about history painting than anything else. I wanted to create an environment in which the paintings could function as parodies of history painting, and in which comments could be made about current social and political situations.[10]

At one level, Birk's installation can be read as an elaborate spoof of the American public's obsession

... and the Heroes Fell on Fulton, 1996. Ink on Paper, 8 x 6 inches. Collection Jess H. Ghannam.

with the Civil War, and the vast industry — books, magazine articles, films, TV documentaries and dramas, museums, theme parks, historic sites and Web sites, clubs, souvenirs and memorabilia — that panders to and inflames that fixation.

At another level, Birk's saga plays on the inane yet persistent cultural, ideological, and economic rivalry between Northern and Southern California. Southern Californians scoff at Northern California's pretensions to cultural superiority, its provincial *hauteur* and unjustifiably smug self-satisfaction; Northern Californians despise Southern California's crass philistinism, mass-media pop culture, and the theft of their water supply. Embedded in Birk's canvases are hot political and economic issues between North and South that might serve as motivations for a war: water rights, Valley secession, immigration, pollution, commerce, even movie deals.

If museums exist to collect, preserve, and display artifacts that reveal and define societies and cultures, what does Birk's museum tell us about ours?

It memorializes, with deadpan reverence, a pointless, anarchic, hugely destructive, to-the-death turf struggle among the proletariat. *The Great War* is *not* about a glorious bid for liberty, equality, and fraternity. Read between the lines, look beneath the varnish on the canvas, and you become aware of a dystopic scenario not unlike that forecast by political science writer Robert D. Kaplan in his new book, *The Coming Anarchy* : "a new kind of global anarchy instigated by poverty, swelling populations and a culture of militarized gangsterism and transnational corporations . . . taking shape under our very noses [and] . . . .likely to change forever the world of stable nation-states with stable borders that most of us have come to see as . . . permanent."[11]

The Great War is a meta-exhibition: a comedic yet impassioned examination of the illusion industry, its institutions, and the iconographies of propaganda, whether disguised as high art, mass media entertainment, religious symbolism, political persuasion or corporate advertising. False history masquerading as lighthearted satire, it acknowledges serious social ills and conjures a horrific vision of the not-so-distant future. Birk's images are stand-ins for contemporary TV docudramas, network newscasts, Hollywood feature films, and product advertising: all the dazzling "dys-entertainment'" that distract us from what's really going on.

Those in power, Birk implies, have always used imagery and language to create myths and seductive illusions that persuade the masses to believe, to be manipulated and controlled. *In Smog and Thunder* is less a goofy celebration of a civil war than a covert call for revolution.

Independent curator, art critic, and writer Marcia Tanner grew up in Los Angeles and has lived in the San Francisco Bay area for twenty-five years. The Great War of the Californias is the story of her life.

The Storming of the Redoubts on Potrero Hill, 1996. Ink on Paper, 15 x 12 inches. Collection Jess H. Ghannam.

[1] Ralph Rugoff, *Circus Americanus*, (London and New York: Verso Press, 1995), x.

[2] *Ibid.*, xi.

[3] Besides Mark Tansey, a number of contemporary artists parody history paintings as a strategy for social and cultural critique, including Robert Colescott, Kara Walker, Komar and Melamid, and Nicole Eisenman. Colescott's cartoonish canvases incorporate the sleazy, racist stereotypes missing from older versions, while Komar and Melamid mock the empty posturing and grandiose vacuity of Soviet Socialist Realism.

[4] Marcia Tucker, *"Bad" Painting* (New York: The New Museum, 1978), exhib. cat., n.p.

[5] From Birk's e-mail to the author, 16 February 2000.

[6] The 1999 exhibition *The Museum as Muse* at the Museum of Modern Art in New York assembled work in this vein by scores of twentieth-century artists, including Marcel Duchamp, Hans Haacke, Louise Lawler, Fred Wilson, Christian Boltanski, and Barbara Bloom. For *Museum Pieces: Bay Area Artists Consider the de Young* – a recent exhibition at the M.H. de Young Memorial Museum in San Francisco (January-March, 2000) – eighteen San Francisco Bay Area artists were commissioned to produce work focusing on the changing role of the museum in society. Since 1984, Los Angeles has been home to the Museum of Jurassic Technology, a unique institution whose carefully constructed "labyrinth of confusion" [Rugoff, *op. cit.*, p. 100] turns the museum experience into an existential confidence game that totally confounds viewers' ability to distinguish between history and fiction, information and disinformation, science and art.

[7] Tucker, *op. cit.*, 1978, n.p.

[8] Umberto Eco, "Travels in Hyperreality," in *Travels in Hyperreality* (San Diego, New York and London: Harcourt Brace Jovanovich, 1986), 58.

[9] *Ibid.*, 9-10.

[10] From Birk's e-mail to the author, 20 February 2000.

[11] Richard Bernstein, "Dashing Short-lived Hopes of Global Harmony," review of *The Coming Anarchy: Shattering the Dreams of the Post-Cold War*," by Robert D. Kaplan, The *New York Times*, 23 February 2000, B9.

An Incident from the Battle of Los Angeles, 1998. Ink on Paper, 17 x 14 inches. Courtesy of Catharine Clark Gallery, San Francisco, California.

California Painting In a Different Light: A Portrait of Sandow Birk

by Tyler Stallings

OUTSIDE

Birk's peripatetic years in Latin America and Europe have provided the foundation for both his artwork and his view of the artist's role in society. Able to speak Portuguese, Spanish, and some French, Birk became a fascinated observer of local customs and art forms. His wanderings – eventually supported by prestigious grants — allowed him to step outside his native California culture and outside prevailing notions of appropriate styles and subjects for contemporary art.

Birk was eighteen years old in 1981 when he began his art training at Otis Art Institute of Parsons School of Design (now Otis College of Art and Design) in Los Angeles. Two years later, he dropped out to travel with a friend to Rio de Janeiro, Brazil, a destination chosen for its good surfing.

To make the trip into a real adventure, Birk and his friend decided to drive from Los Angeles to Rio via the Transcontinental Highway. Their jeep made it as far as Central America; after that, they took a bus that stopped in every village. Birk and his friend figured their skill in making surfboards – developed in after-school school jobs back home in Seal Beach — would be exportable.

And sure enough, they discovered they were able to make a living by hooking up with the local surfboard maker in each coastal hamlet. Birk's specialty was lamination; his friend did the shaping. After a few days, they would move on, but not before learning where to find a surfboard shaper in the next village. Their cash reserves were down to $150 by time they got to Rio, six months later, but they immediately found jobs in surfboard factories.

In the fall of 1984, Birk decided to study in Europe for a year. He spent one semester on an exchange program at Parsons in Paris and then transferred to another college in Bath, England — chosen specifically because the city was fairly near the coast, and he could surf on the weekends.

Studying with students from around the world at the American College in Paris, Birk was blown away by the experience of looking at nineteenth-century paintings in the Louvre. "The scale,

The Midnight Assault on the Getty, 1998. Ink on Paper, 17 x 14 inches. Courtesy Catharine Clark Gallery, San Francisco, California.

the cinematic quality, and the virtuosity made painting seem important and thrilling, [as opposed to] the bland conceptualism I was seeing in L.A.," he says.

He also had memorable skateboarding experiences in Europe. Zooming through the streets and subways of Paris all night long, Birk remembers,

"was great because skating was new there and there weren't laws against it yet. Cops were confused by it. And there were so many great places to skate, especially when they drained all of the fountains in the winter to keep them from cracking. We skated the big fountains in the center of the Place de la Concorde, the duck ponds under the Eiffel Tower, the parking structures at London's South Bank museum...."

This sense of intimacy with urban environments would infuse Birk's first serious paintings and all of his subsequent work, including *Tales of the City* and *The Great War of the Californias*.

After the year in Europe, Birk returned to Rio, expecting to remain only for the summer and then return to art school in Los Angeles. But he was offered a job as art director at the Brazilian edition of *Surfer Magazine* and wound up staying two years.

"I worked illegally," Birk says. "At one time, my boss tried to figure out ways to make it easier, like marrying this woman he knew. I was suppose to leave the country every three months, but the border was about fifteen hours away, so I never did."

Life as an illegal alien, a unique experience for a U.S. citizen, would inform Birk's later thematic explorations of border issues and ethnic tension, especially in *The Great War of the Californias* series.

Birk's return to Rio also was significant for him as an artist. He started painting for himself for the first time, as opposed to doing class assignments, and he began to realize that adhering too closely to academic notions about art could obscure its role as a cultural marker. Many of his new works depicted nocturnal scenes in airports, hotel rooms, and train stations, recalled from years of traipsing about in two hemispheres. In the late '80s, he began painting these scenes on velvet – partly as an homage to the kitsch art he had seen in Brazilian villages.

Birk returned to Los Angeles in 1987 to finish his BFA at Otis/Parsons. After his experiences abroad, he had a new self-confidence and thought of himself more as a professional artist than as a student. His most influential teachers — Jill Giegerich, John Mandel, Michael Davis, Gary Panter, and Carole Caroompas – all stressed conceptual thinking over technique.

After graduating in spring 1989, he rented a storefront near the intersection of Adams and Crenshaw boulevards in South-Central L.A., an area that would become the subject of much of Birk's work. The contradictions involved in being a white artist living and working in a black neighborhood would have some odd consequences later in his career.

The Ambush of the Four-Level, 1998. Ink on Paper, 17 x 14 inches. Courtesy Koplin Gallery, Los Angeles, California.

MARITIME

Birk's press releases and reviews often include a seemingly condescending reference to his love of surfing, as if the gallery or critic is saying, "Look, the dumb surfer can paint." Surfing magazine articles, on the other hand, exude pride at seeing one of their own succeed. Birk takes all this in stride, happily flouting two stereotypes: the dumb surfer and the brooding artist.

For years, he had thought about painting surfing scenes, to show the sport as a serious activity instead of a frivolous, teenage pastime. After all, surfing is not as spontaneous as outsiders might assume. Before hitting the waves, you have to know weather patterns, watch the tides, and read maps. It is actually a serious maritime activity, on par with navigating a boat.

Birk's recognition of surfing as part of a larger context of maritime history helped crystallize his new approach in the '90s: updating the compositions of old master paintings he had seen in European museums with twentieth-century scenes. He began doing riffs on such works as Théodore Géricault's *The Raft of the "Medusa"* and Emanuel Leutze's *Washington Crossing the Delaware*, replacing the historical figures with surfers in the throes of both a past and present history.

Looking at old marine paintings, which occupied a much lower rung in the traditional hierarchy than history paintings or portraiture, Birk realized that the second-class status of images of seagoing vessels paralleled the reaction of the art world to surfing.

Realizing that he didn't have the chops to emulate nineteenth-century painters like J.M.W. Turner, Fitz Hugh Lane, and Martin Johnson Heade, Birk decided simply to borrow their compositions. He projected the original image onto a canvas, traced it, and then painted the figures in his own style, adding the surfing element as a final, contemporary touch.

In *The Purchase of Manhattan* (1991), a painting from his first surfing series, *Birth of a Surf Nation*, Birk borrows from *"Landing of William Penn"* by early nineteenth-century painter Thomas Birch. We see Penn speaking with a Mohawk Indian, ostensibly making the deal of the millennium, with twentieth-century Manhattan in the background. There's a surfboard in the foreground and a goat wearing a tire — a quote from Robert Rauschenberg's 1959 combine painting, *Monogram*. Birk raises the issues of fair trade and colonialism. Whose history will be remembered, the white man's or the Indian's?

TAG

Along with work that fused ancient and contemporary mariners, Birk turned his attention to the more land-locked environment of downtown L.A. in *Tales of the City*, whose title was inspired by Charles Dickens' novel, *A Tale of Two Cities*.

This series, produced between 1992 and 1995, deals with gang warfare and the urban environment in general. Birk returned to the nocturnal ambiance of the Rio paintings, but set this

The Collapse of the Master Gardener, 1998. Ink on Paper, 17 x 14 inches. Collection Paul Zaloom.

work in his South-Central L.A.neighborhood, where he constantly heard gunshots and often had to lie on the floor to avoid stray bullets.

The series included collaborations with taggers and graffiti artists Birk had met in the neighborhood. His interest was not so much in what the images represent as in the parallels between the academy-trained art world and the world of street artists. He was intrigued by the Renaissance-style apprentice system necessary to produce a site-specific, mural-size work in minutes. A young graffiti artist would start out filling in the backgrounds and then graduate to creating major portions of a piece.

Birk suddenly viewed his study of European art history through different eyes. He observed that graffiti artists are known more for the location of their work than their painting skill. (Ser, for example, is supposedly the first guy in L.A. to tag the back of a freeway sign.) By emphasizing process over product, these artists parallel aspects of Conceptualism. The letters in the tags, often twisted and bent to the point of non-recognition, also become a form of abstract imagery.

Tales of the City also deals with gang violence, especially the feuds between the Bloods and Crips. Birk often depicts the gangbangers against a graffiti backdrop, in a tableau based on a historical painting. For example, *The Duel* (in collaboration with Devin "REALM" Flynn) quotes Jean-Léon Gérôme's *Duel After the Masquerade*. In the updated version, a Crip held by three friend dies as a tire iron slips from his hand. Birk contrasts the mythic, heroic quality of the nineteenth-century work with the vernacular imagery of the inner-city scene. For all their differences, both deaths are romanticized.

Many artists have used this composition, based on the Pietà, the image of the Virgin Mary mourning the dead body of Christ. Benjamin West, a Romantic painter eager to give a factual yet ennobling account of a contemporary scene of military heroism, used the composition for *The Death of General Wolfe* (1770). Birk, on the other hand, does not intend his Pietà quotation to cast a heroic light on gang warfare. Rather, he underlines the mythic qualities surrounding 'heroic' deaths, whether they are religious, nationalistic, or about turf battles in troubled neighborhoods.

Three weeks after the first exhibition of works from this series opened in 1992 at Bess Cutler Gallery, riots followed the acquittal of four white Los Angeles Police Department officers in the beating of black motorist Rodney King. The paintings were full of teeming crowd scenes and large-scale destruction. Magazine editors looking for illustrations for riot coverage marveled at Birk's prescience.

Perhaps unsurprisingly, the subject matter led people to assume that he was black. Writers for mainstream magazines were disappointed when they came to his studio and discovered that he was a white Anglo, not even a Latino. ("Sandow" is his mother's maiden name; his parents think it may be of German or Irish origin.) A dealer told him that a collector who directed "boyz in the hood"-style films was about to buy a piece but changed his mind when he found out that Birk was not black.

Criticized for painting a world in which he was judged an interloper, Birk argued that he simply painted what he saw. Of course, there is a valid argument that despite Birk's sincere intentions, his skin color allows him to co-opt the trials and tribulations of a minority group. It is an ongoing debate.

The Heaving of Major Appliances During the Assault on the Getty, 1998. Ink on Paper, 17 x 14 inches. Collection Marcia Tanner.

Sandow Birk's "In Smog and Thunder: Historical Works from The Great War of the Californias" reflects many of the experiences Birk had in Latin America and Europe: discovering the similarities and disparities between the two hemispheres; being an illegal alien; and becoming intimately familiar with the smallest details of a city.

What determines if an artist is representing an authentic history? What is art history? Exploring these questions is at the crux of Birk's recent series, *The Great War of the Californias*. In this work he refers to a different kind of essentialism, one based on geographical boundaries rather than skin color.

Birk thinks of his work as a museum display for visitors who share a common history, much as the Gettysburg Museum in Pennsylvania presupposes some knowledge of the Civil War. Of course, it is precisely this ambiguity that leads viewers to think about all the issues in the work. People always want to know, Who wins the war? Birk hints at the possibility that Los Angeles is the victor, but only with the help of reinforcements from Tijuana. Slyly, he notes that the imaginary museum from which all of the work has been loaned for *The Great War of the Californias* is based in Tijuana.

But Birk does not present the viewer with an us-versus-them situation. Through the use of details specific to each city and region (like the particular style of street lights on Wilshire Boulevard in Los Angeles), he gives you an experience akin to returning home after a long trip, newly aware of your familiar surroundings. By this means, Birk allows the viewer to feel part of the story, equally sympathetic to all parties in the struggle.

Birk's brand of ironic narrative painting has never been associated with Southern California, home of Light and Space, Finish Fetish, and new forms of landscape and Color Field painting. And yet, he deals with hot-button California issues, including ethnic identity, illegal aliens, and the threatened secession of the San Fernando Valley from L.A. His work is quintessentially Californian because he treats the artifacts of today's world as points of intersection for the multiple voices, styles, and attitudes that make up our state's culture.

Charging the Line, 1998. Ink on Paper, 17 x 14 inches. Collection Angela and Gerald Harrington.

WORKS IN THE EXHIBITION

All dimensions in inches, height preceding width.

Battle Scenes

Scene from the Desolation: Los Angeles County Museum of Art, 1995
Oil and acrylic on canvas
12 x 19
Collection Harry L. Tarnoff

Scene from the Desolation: 7-11, 1995
Oil and acrylic on canvas
12 x 19
Private Collection

The Battle of San Francisco Bay, 1996
Oil on canvas
34 x 57
Collection Lane Schofield

The Final Hours of Telegraph Hill, 1996
Oil on canvas
43 x 54
Collection Barbara DeZonia

The Great Battle of San Francisco, 1996
Oil on canvas
84 x 84
Rene & Veronica di Rosa Foundation,
Napa, California

Memorial to the Battle of San Francisco,
1996
Oil on canvas
54 x 34
Collection Ryszard Koprowski

Rendezvous at Twin Peaks, 1996
Oil on canvas
50 x 50
Collection Paul Stephen Price

San Francisco on the Ruins of Her City, 1996
Oil on canvas
54 x 34
Collection Marsha and Darrel Anderson

Surprise Strike from the Sea, 1997
Oil on canvas
34 x 57
Collection Catherine and Brent Brouwer

Air Supremacy, 1998
Oil on canvas
32 x 22
Collection Dean Ziehl

Air Supremacy (The Battle of the Bay), 1998
Oil on canvas
45 x 45
Courtesy Koplin Gallery, Los Angeles

Allegory of The Great War of the Californias,
1998
Oil on canvas
43 x 54
Collection Eileen Natuzzi, M.D.

The Bombardment of San Pedro, 1998
Oil on canvas
43 x 54
Collection Marcela and Greg Phillips

The Destruction of the LAS Tinsel Town *by
the SFS* Republic of San Francisco, 1998
Oil on canvas
24 x 48
Collection Christopher Gaebler

The Great Battle of Los Angeles, 1998
Oil on canvas
64 x 120
Collection Louis and Helene Galen

Los Angeles Triumphant, 1998
Oil on canvas
54 x 43
Collection Donald R. Boulanger

The Spirit of Los Angeles, 1998
Oil on canvas
54 x 43
Courtesy Koplin Gallery, Los Angeles

The Triumph of the "San Francisco", 1998
Oil on canvas
90 x 134
Courtesy Catharine Clark Gallery,
San Francisco

Fictional Portraits

Portrait of Lt. Quincy Salerno, 1996
Oil on canvas
30 x 22
Collection Jess H. Ghannam

*Portrait of Maj. Gen. Juan Gomez
de los Angeles,* 1996
Oil on canvas
30 x 22
Courtesy Koplin Gallery,
Los Angeles

Portrait of Col. Don Ho Park, 1998
Oil on canvas
30 x 22
Courtesy Koplin Gallery, Los Angeles

Portrait of Field Commander Toma-Agua,
1998
Oil on canvas
32 x 22
Courtesy Catharine Clark Gallery,
San Francisco

Portrait of Gen. Felix Hernandez, 1998
Oil on canvas
32 x 22
Collection Basil Alkazzi

Portrait of Lt. Comdr. Rebecca Jordan,
1998
Oil on canvas
32 x 22
Collection Jess H. Ghannam

The Floundering Fleet, 1998. Ink on Paper, 17 x 14 inches. Collection Grafton Tanquary.

Portrait of Lt. Maj. DJ Downs, 1998
Oil on canvas
32 x 22
Collection Paul and Jill Koplin

Unfinished Portrait (LA), 1998
Oil on canvas
24 x 22
Collection Julian Ysais

Unfinished Portrait (SF), 1998
Oil on canvas
24 x 22
Courtesy Catharine Clark Gallery,
San Francisco

Drawings

... and the Heroes Fell on Fulton, 1996
Ink on paper
8 x 6
Collection Jess H. Ghannam

The Bloody Defense of Telegraph Hill,
1996
Ink on paper
16 x 22
Collection Ryszard Koprowski

The Last Defense of the Coit Tower, 1996
Ink on paper
8 x 6
Courtesy Catharine Clark Gallery,
San Francisco

Last Stand in the Marina, 1996
Ink on paper
11 x 9
Collection Judy and Sheldon Greene

*The Rest of the Fallen in the Richmond
District,* 1996
Ink on paper
11 x 9
Courtesy Catharine Clark Gallery,
San Francisco

The Revenge of San Francisco, 1996
Ink on paper
8 x 6
Collection J. O. Bugental

San Francisco Avenger, 1996
Ink on paper
11 x 9
Courtesy Catharine Clark Gallery,
San Francisco

Skirmishes South of Market, 1996
Ink on paper
16 x 22
Collection Ryszard Koprowski

The Storming of the Redoubts on Potrero Hill,
1996
Ink on paper
11 x 9
Collection Jess H. Ghannam

After the Battle for the Rose Bowl, 1998
Ink on paper
17 x 14
From the Judy and Stuart Spence
Collection

The Ambush at the Four Level, 1998
Ink on paper
17 x 14
Courtesy Koplin Gallery, Los Angeles

Charging the Line, 1998
Ink on paper
17 x 14
Collection Angela and Gerald Harrington

The Collapse of the Master Gardener, 1998
Ink on paper
17 x 14
Collection Paul Zaloom

The Defense of the De Young, 1998
Ink on paper
17 x 14
Collection Ryszard Koprowski

The Desperate Charge of the 101, 1998
Ink on paper
17 x 14
Courtesy Koplin Gallery, Los Angeles

The Floundering Fleet, 1998
Ink on paper
17 x 14
Collection Grafton Tanquary

The Heaving of Major Appliances..., 1998
Ink on paper
17 x 14
Collection Grafton Tanquary

An Incident from the Battle for Los Angeles,
1998
Ink on paper
17 x 14
Courtesy Koplin Gallery, Los Angeles

Los Angeles Defiant, 1998
Ink on paper
17 x 14
Collection Brenda, Gary, and Harrison
Ruttenberg

The March of Commerce, 1998
Ink on paper
17 x 14
Collection Angela and Gerald Harrington

The Massacre of the Innocents, 1998
Ink on paper
17 x 14
Collection Grafton Tanquary

The Midnight Assault on the Getty, 1998
Ink on paper
17 x 14
Courtesy Koplin Gallery, Los Angeles

Reinforcements Arriving Too Late..., 1998
Ink on paper
17 x 14
From the Stuart and Judy Spence
Collection

The March of Commerce, 1998. Ink on Paper, 17 x 14 inches. Collection Angela and Gerald Harrington.

*The Skater's Confession
(The Great Battle of Los Angeles)*, 1998
Mixed media
17 x 14
Courtesy Koplin Gallery, Los Angeles

The Bombardment of the Getty Center,
1999
Ink on paper
39 x 78
Collection Jill and Jonathan Fink

Shallow History and the Razing of Icons,
2000
Pencil and acrylic on paper
39 x 78
Collection Les Firestein

Faux Posters

Cultural Terror, 1998
Acrylic on paper
38 x 25
Collection Isabel and David Breskin

For the City, My Eyes . . . Angelenos Unite,
1998
Acrylic on paper
38 x 25
Collection Philip E. Thomas

HANDS OFF L.A.!, 1998
Acrylic on paper
38 x 25
Collection Michael Davis

HELP STOP THIS!, 1998
Acrylic on paper
38 x 25
Courtesy Koplin Gallery, Los Angeles

Homeless Veterans Assistance Program, 1998
Acrylic on paper
38 x 25
Courtesy Catharine Clark Gallery,
San Francisco

Los Angeles the Devourer, 1998
Acrylic on paper
38 x 25
Courtesy Catharine Clark Gallery,
San Francisco

Porno Wanted for Our Men in Camp, 1998
Acrylic on paper
38 x 25
Collection Isabel and David Breskin

San Franciscan–The Seas Are Ours!, 1998
Acrylic on paper
38 x 25
Collection Isabel and David Breskin

SMASH THE SOUTH!, 1998
Acrylic on paper
38 x 25
Courtesy Koplin Gallery, Los Angeles

Sociedad General de Veteranos de la Guerra,
1998
Acrylic on paper
38 x 25
Courtesy Catharine Clark Gallery,
San Francisco

Staking The Prize, 1998
Acrylic on paper
38 x 25
Collection Judy and Sheldon Greene

Stop This Monster, 1998
Acrylic on paper
38 x 25
Courtesy Catharine Clark Gallery,
San Francisco

The Three Headed Monster of the North,
1998
Acrylic on paper
38 x 25
Lynn and John Pleshette Collection

Sculptures

Sandow Birk and Stephen Rivers
Map of the Great Battle of San Francisco,
1996
Mixed media
40 x 48 x 40
Rene & Veronica di Rosa Foundation,
Napa, California

Sandow Birk and Kevin Ancell
The Battleship San Francisco, 1998
Mixed media
55 x 132 x 42
Courtesy Catharine Clark Gallery,
San Francisco

Sandow Birk and Stephen Rivers
Map of the Great Battle of Los Angeles,
1998
Mixed media
40 x 48 x 40
Courtesy Catharine Clark Gallery,
San Francisco

Sailboat #1, 1998
Mixed media
5 x 7 x 2
Courtesy Catharine Clark Gallery,
San Francisco

Sailboat #2, 1998
Mixed media
5 x 7 x 2
Courtesy Catharine Clark Gallery,
San Francisco

Submarine, 1998
Mixed media
11 x 7 x 3
Courtesy Catharine Clark Gallery,
San Francisco

Untitled Models–Helicopters, 1998
Mixed media
6 x 8 x 4 each (6 pieces)
Courtesy Catharine Clark Gallery,
San Francisco

The Defense of the De Young, 1998. Ink on Paper, 17 x 14 inches. Collection Ryszard Koprowski.

Untitled Models–Jet Fighters, 1998
Mixed media
5 x 7 x 8 each (6 pieces)
Courtesy Catharine Clark Gallery,
San Francisco

Untitled Warship (American Express), 1998
Mixed media
26 x 20 x 9
Courtesy Catharine Clark Gallery,
San Francisco, California

Untitled Warship (ATM card), 1998
Mixed media
22 x 22 x 8
Courtesy Catharine Clark Gallery,
San Francisco

Untitled Warship (IBM), 1998
Mixed media
22 x 22 x 8
Courtesy Catharine Clark Gallery,
San Francisco

Untitled Warship (MasterCard), 1998
Mixed media
27 x 20 x 7
Courtesy Catharine Clark Gallery,
San Francisco

Untitled Warship (VISA), 1998
Mixed media
25 x 18 x 8
Courtesy Catharine Clark Gallery,
San Francisco

The Warship Los Angeles, 1998
Mixed media
22 x 24 x 8
Courtesy Catharine Clark Gallery,
San Francisco

The Battleship Tinsel Town, 2000
Mixed media
50 x 138 x 38
Courtesy Koplin Gallery,
Los Angeles, California

The R. M. Nixon, 2000
Mixed media
40 x 74 x 25
Courtesy Koplin Gallery,
Los Angeles, California

59

Shallow History and the Razing of Icons, 2000. Acrylic and Pencil on Paper, 39 x 78 inches framed. Collection Les Firestein. 12

60

Selected Biography & Bibliography

b. 1962, Detroit, Michigan

EDUCATION

1988	BFA, Otis Art Institute of Parson's School of Design, Los Angeles, California
1985	Bath Academy of Art, Bath, England
1984 - 1985	American College in Paris/Parson's School of Design, Paris, France

AWARDS

1999	J. Paul Getty Fellowship for the Visual Arts
1998	The Basil H. Alkazzi Award
1997	Fulbright Grant, Rio de Janeiro, Brazil
1995	Guggenheim Fellowship National Endowment for the Arts, U.S./Mexico International Exchange Scholarship
1994	Western States Art Foundation/National Endowment for the Arts Grant Art Matters Individual Artist Grant

SOLO EXHIBITIONS

2000
Historical Works from The Great War of the Californias, Laguna Art Museum, Laguna Beach, California
Sandow Birk: New Work, Koplin Gallery, Los Angeles, California

Historical Works from the Stonewall Riots and Beyond, Catharine Clark Gallery, San Francisco, California

1999
Carioca: A Year Among the Natives of Rio de Janeiro, San Jose Museum of Art, California
Historical Works from the Stonewall Riots and Beyond, Earl McGrath Gallery, New York, New York
Sandow Birk: New Work, Catharine Clark Gallery, San Francisco, California

1998
Smog and Thunder: Historical Works from The War of the Californias, (Part I), Catherine Clark Gallery, San Francisco, California
Smog and Thunder: Historical Works from The War of the Californias (Part II), Koplin Gallery, Los Angeles, California

1997
Carioca: A Year Among the Natives of Rio de Janeiro, Laguna Art Museum, Laguna Beach, California, traveled to San Jose Museum of Art, San Jose, California
Skatistas, Moleques, Mendigos (Skaters, Punks, Street Kids): New Drawings from Rio de Janeiro by Sandow Birk, Spruce Street Forum Gallery, San Diego, California

1996
Historical Paintings of the Great Battle of San Francisco, Catharine Clark Gallery, San Francisco, California
Sandow Birk: Recent Work, Michael Solway Gallery, Cincinnati, Ohio

1995
Chilangos: Drawings by Sandow Birk and *The Rise and Fall of Los Angeles: New Work by Sandow Birk*, Koplin Gallery, Santa Monica, California
Sandow Birk, Centro Nacional de las Artes, Mexico City, D.F.
Tales of the Cities: New Paintings by Sandow Birk, Morphos Gallery, San Francisco, California

1994
Skaters: New Drawings by Sandow Birk, Koplin Gallery, Santa Monica, California
Asphalt Landscape: Recent Paintings by Sandow Birk, Carl Hammer Gallery, Chicago, Illinois

1993
Truce: Sandow Birk, Julie Rico Gallery, Santa Monica, California

1992
The Gates of Hell: L.A. Landscapes of the '90s, Orange Coast College, Costa Mesa, California
Sandow Birk, Bess Cutler Gallery, Santa Monica, California

1990
New Velvet: New Paintings by Sandow Birk, Earl McGrath Gallery, Los Angeles, California

1989
Velvet: Sandow Birk, Earl McGrath Gallery, Los Angeles, California

SELECTED GROUP EXHIBITIONS

2000

Fact or Fiction: Contemporary Art that Walks the Line, San Francisco Museum of Modern Art, San Francisco, California

Made in California: 1900-2000, Los Angeles County Museum of Art, Los Angeles, California

1999

Surfin' Art, South Texas Institute for the Arts, Corpus Christi, Texas

When Borders Migrate: Reflections on the 150th Anniversary of the Treaty of Guadalupe Hidalgo, The Museum of Art and History, Santa Cruz, California

Courting the Muse: Contemporary Paintings, Historical Influences, Main Gallery, Cal State Fullerton, Fullerton, California

62 *1998*

Contingent Reality, Diane Nelson Gallery, Laguna Beach, California

Skate Lore: California Skate(board)ing Index to Concepts, Forms, Life, Santa Barbara Contemporary Arts Center, Santa Barbara, California

Tribute to La Luz de Jesus Gallery, Track 16 Gallery, Santa Monica, California

1997

Lineas de Correspondencia, Galeria José Maria Velasco, Instituto Nacional de Bellas Artes, Mexico City, D.F.

1996

RE: Masters: New Images from Old Sources, Rancho Santiago College, Santa Ana, California

Melody Makers, Gallerie Torta di Miele, Bologna, Italy

Drawn from L.A.: Drawings by Contemporary Artists, Armory Center for the Arts, Pasadena, California

Paintings of the New Landscape, Peter Blake Gallery, Laguna Beach, California

1995

It's Only Rock 'n' Roll, Phoenix Art Museum, Arizona; Tacoma Art Museum, Tacoma, Washington; Contemporary Arts Center, Cincinnati, Ohio; and others

Social Engagement, City of Los Angeles Municipal Art Gallery, Los Angeles, California

1994

The Night of the Masque, Newport Harbor Art Museum, Newport Beach, California

1993

Surf Show, Julie Rico Gallery, Santa Monica, California

Kustom Kulture: Von Dutch, Ed "Big Daddy" Roth, Robert Williams & Others, Laguna Art Museum, Laguna Beach, California

1992

East Meets West, Speedway Gallery, Boston, Massachusetts

I Thought California Would Be Different, Laguna Art Museum, Laguna Beach, California

1991

Post-Pop And Beyond, Bess Cutler Gallery, Santa Monica, California

Synthetic History, Parker-Zanik Gallery, Los Angeles, California

SELECTED BIBLIOGRAPHY

Andersen, Marchesini. "Art That Will Rip Your Heart Out," *Torta di Miele* (Bologna, Italy) November 1994: 12-16.

Anderson, Ross. "War of the Californias." *Panik Magazine* 6, no. 1 (November 1998): 7-8.

"Artworld: Awards." *Art in America* (March 1999): 156.

Asch, Andrew. "Sandow Birk: Connected to the Canvas." *The Orange County Register*, 9 November 1997.

Brisick, Jamie. "God is Brazilian." *Surfing Magazine* (November 1997): 126.

———. "Paint By Fate: Sandow Birk." *Surfing Magazine* (April 1996): 122.

———. "Sandow Birk." *Juxtapoz Art Quarterly* (July 1996): 37-42.

Clark, Orville, Jr. "Sandow Birk at Koplin." *ArtScene* 18, no. 11 (September 1998): 11.

Colburn, Bolton. "In the Heroic Tradition: Sandow Birk." *Surfer's Journal* (fall 1992): 24-32.

Curtis, Cathy. "The More Things Change...'Updating' the Grand Masters: Sandow Birk Looks Back to the Present." *Los Angeles Times,* 17 September, 1992.

Diez, Héctor León. "Correspondence Lines: An Artistic Bridge between Mexico and the U.S.," *La Cronica de Hoy* (Mexico City), 1 July 1997.

Farr, Michael. "South Seas, Please." *International Tattoo Art Magazine* (March 1999): 122-123.

Frank, Peter. "Pick of the Week." *L.A. Weekly*, 23-29 October, 1998.

Geer, Suvan. "Sandow Birk's Velvets." *Los Angeles Times*, 1 September 1989.

Gleason, Matt. "City Beat: Birk and Ocampo," *Most Art Sucks*. Santa Monica: Small Art Press. 1998.

Gunnin, John. "Surfin' the 'Hood: The Art of Sandow Birk." *Art? Alternatives* (spring 1994): 32-37.

Helfand, Glen. "When Borders Migrate." *San Francisco Bay Guardian*, 4 February 1998.

Isé, Claudine. "Sly Scenes Picture a California Engulfed in Civil War." *Los Angeles Times*, 16 October 1998.

Kandel, Susan. "Birk's Best." *Los Angeles Times*, 29 September 1994.

La Brecque, Eric. "L.A. Aftermath: The Graphic Response to the L.A. Riots." *Print Magazine* (September/October 1993): 24-25.

Lenkert, Erika. "L.A. to Z: Artist Sandow Birk." *Los Angeles Magazine* (December 1998): 107.

Marcus, Greil. "Flotsam and Jetsam of the Calif. State of Mind." *The New York Times*, 30 March 1998.

Matthies, Eric. "Sandow Birk at Spruce Street Forum." *Giant Robot Magazine*, no. 9 (winter 1997): 54.

Meyers, Holly. "Sandow Birk at Koplin Gallery." *Art issues.* (November/December 1998): 37.

Ortiz-Torres, Rubén, guest ed. "Portfolio: Sandow Birk." *Poliester Magazine* (Mexico City, D.F.) 7, no. 25 (summer 1999): 51.

Pincus, Robert. "Airborne: Sandow Birk at Spruce Gallery." *San Diego Union Tribune*, 19 June 1997.

Reed, Michale. "The Art Academy." *Artweek* 30, no. 3 (March 1999): 81.

Robertson, Jean and Craig McDaniel. *Painting As Language*. Fort Worth, Texas: Harcourt Brace, 2000.

Ribeiro, Vavá. "A Perigosa Verdade (The Dangerous Truth)." *Revista Trip* (São Paulo, Brazil) 10, no. 56 (1997): 123-124.

Ruben, David S. *It's Only Rock-and-Roll: Currents in Contemporary Art*. New York: Prestel, 1995.

"Sandow Birk: Drawings," *Zyzzyva* 13, no.1 (spring 1997): 155-158.

"Sandow Birk: Drawings," *Zyzzyva* 12, no. 1 (spring 1996): 146-149.

Scarborough, James. "Los Angeles, Prophet and Loss." *Art Press 184 International Magazine* (Paris) October 1993.

Schoenkopf, Rebecca. "It's Relative." *OC Weekly* (12 March 1999): 25.

Stamets, Bill. "Painters Put Slant on News." *Chicago Sun-Times*, 16 April, 1994.

Tanner, Marcia. "Sandow Birk at Catherine Clark." *Artweek* (March 1997): 52-53.

"Ten to Watch in 1993." *Details* (January 1993): 84.

Turner, John. *Leeteg of Tahiti: Paintings from the Villa Velour.* San Francisco: Last Gasp Press, 1999.

Turner, Fredrick. "The Landscape of Disturbance." *The Wilson Quarterly* (spring 1998): 37.

Urban, Hope. "Art 'n' the Hood: Paintings of and by the Street Youth of Los Angeles." *Visions Art Quarterly* (winter 1993): 51-52.

Willett, J.M.S. "Bad Boys/Good Boys: Sandow Birk and the Killing of Los Angeles." *Visions Art Quarterly* (fall 1992): 47-49.

"Works on Paper: Sandow Birk." *Zyzzyva*, 14, no. 3 (winter 1998): 97-100.

64